The Hun
of Notre

Victor Hugo

Abridged and adapted by Steven Osborn

Illustrated by Carol Stutz

A PACEMAKER CLASSIC

GLOBE FEARON
Pearson Learning Group

Pacemaker Classics

The Adventures of Huckleberry Finn
The Adventures of Tom Sawyer
The Call of the Wild
A Christmas Carol
Crime and Punishment
David Copperfield
The Deerslayer
Dr. Jekyll and Mr. Hyde
Ethan Frome
Frankenstein
Great Expectations
Heart of Darkness
The Hunchback of Notre Dame
Jane Eyre
The Jungle Book
The Last of the Mohicans

The Mayor of Casterbridge
Moby Dick
The Moonstone
O Pioneers!
The Prince and the Pauper
The Red Badge of Courage
Robinson Crusoe
The Scarlet Letter
A Tale of Two Cities
The Three Musketeers
The Time Machine
Treasure Island
20,000 Leagues Under the Sea
Two Years Before the Mast
The War of the Worlds
Wuthering Heights

ISBN 0-8224-9341-1
Printed in the United States of America

9 10 11 12   07 06 05 04 03

1-800-321-3106
www.pearsonlearning.com

Contents

1 The Prince of Fools

It was the morning of January 6th, 1482. A large crowd gathered inside the Palace of Justice in Paris, France. They had come to the great hall to watch a play and to choose the prince of fools. Today was the Feast of Fools, a holiday. Every year on this day the people of Paris chose their prince of fools. Then the prince would lead a wild parade through the streets of the city.

In 1482, the great hall of the palace was one of the largest rooms in the world. At one end of the hall stood a huge marble table. The slab of marble was so large that it served as the stage for the Feast of Fools play. At the other end was the king's chapel, a type of small church. Above the chapel door was a rose-colored window made of many panes of glass.

Between the chapel and the table stood a large platform covered with gold cloth. The important lords and priests could sit there and watch the play in comfort. The common people had to squeeze together in the rest of the hall. Yet, as large as it was, the great hall could not hold everybody who wanted to get in. Many people stood outside trying to push and shove their way into the hall.

The play was set to begin at noon. Already the crowd was restless. It was almost noon, but Cardinal Bourbon and the other nobles had not arrived. The play could not begin without the cardinal.

Noon came and went. Still the cardinal's velvet armchair stood empty. The crowd started to murmur and then to shout. "The play!" they yelled. "We want to see the play!"

At last an actor appeared on the stage. He cried out, "As you know, the prince of France will soon marry a Flemish princess. Right now the cardinal must attend to these honored guests. He is guiding a group of Flemish lords through our fair city. We will begin as soon as he arrives with the Flemish lords."

"Down with the Flemish!" the mob answered. "Down with the cardinal! Let the play begin!"

The frightened actor did not know what to do. If he began the play, the cardinal would surely hang him. If not, the mob would do the same. He froze in his shoes, fearing for his life.

Just then, a tall, thin, pale young man stepped up to the stage. He spoke to the actor by name. "Michel," he said, "begin the play at once. I'll take the blame if the cardinal is unhappy. We must please the crowd!"

The tall young man was Pierre Gringoire, the

author of the play. He was so anxious to see his play that he was willing to risk the cardinal's anger.

The frightened Michel cried out at the top of his voice, "We will begin at once!" The crowd cheered. Finally the actors took their places. The play began.

Within a few minutes, there was a new delay. From the middle of the hall, the loud voice of the royal usher rang out, "Announcing the great Cardinal Bourbon!"

All eyes turned toward the gold-colored platform. A special door opened, and in walked the handsome cardinal. He was dressed in a flowing red robe. Behind him came a flock of well-dressed bishops and priests. The crowd admired their clothing as the churchmen took their places. Soon the crowd began to settle down.

Then the usher's voice rang out again. "Announcing the Flemish lords!" he cried. Then, two by two, 48 Flemish lords began making their way onto the platform. As they did, the usher called out the names of each and every one. "Jacques de Goy, lord of Dauby! Paul de Baeust, lord of Voirmizelle!" and so on and on, he called.

At last, one final lord approached the platform. He was big and strong but badly dressed. "Your name, sir?" whispered the confused usher.

The lord answered in a booming voice. "My name? Why, I am Jacques Coppenole, the royal tailor!"

The crowd laughed loudly at this news. The cardinal turned up his nose in disgust. But the Flemish lords welcomed their tailor. He was a fun-loving sort who had won a lasting place in their lordly hearts.

What had happened to the play during all this time? Sad to say, the people had forgotten all about it. At first Pierre Gringoire had begged the actors to go on. But then he saw that it was useless. His wonderful play was being ruined by the cardinal and the wretched Flemish lords!

Finally Pierre saw that Jacques Coppenole was the last Flemish lord to reach the platform. He waited for him to be seated, and then he shouted, "The play! On with the play!"

His shouts reached the cardinal's ears. The red-robed lord turned to a servant. "What's all that noise about?" he asked.

"I believe the people want the play to begin," came the answer.

The cardinal yawned. He said, "Oh yes, the play. I had forgotten all about it. Let them begin. I will read my book instead."

The actors began once again. But the play was not very exciting. The crowd soon became bored. The Flemish lords also watched without much interest. The cardinal read his book.

Suddenly, Jacques Coppenole spoke out loudly to

the crowd. "This play is nothing but talk, talk, talk! Where's the action? Where's the fighting? I came here to have fun! Today is the Feast of Fools! I want to pick a prince of fools and have a parade!"

The crowd cheered Coppenole's speech. They, too, had seen enough of the play. Now they wanted action. Pierre Gringoire hid his face in his hands.

Coppenole went on: "Where I come from, we pick the prince of fools by seeing who can make the ugliest face. The winner gets to be the prince. What do you say to that?" he asked. The crowd roared with glee.

Few people noticed the cardinal and his flock quietly leaving the platform. The Feast of Fools parade is no place for a cardinal. He had brought the Flemish lords to the great hall. Now he was glad to be rid of them. He looked forward to reading his book in peace.

Coppenole went on to explain his plan. The people who wanted to be the prince of fools should take turns sticking their heads through the chapel window. Then the crowd should cheer for the ugliest face.

Before long, all eyes turned to the chapel at the end of the great hall. The candidates for the prince of fools had gathered behind the chapel door. Then, one by one, they climbed up to the rose-colored window and stuck their heads through the broken window pane.

The first candidate curled up his eyelids and opened his mouth wide. Then he wrinkled his ugly forehead. The crowd laughed and cheered. But the fun had just begun. The crowd yelled, "That's nothing! Let's have another!"

One after another the candidates appeared. Some drew cheers; others, boos. Then, suddenly, a deafening roar filled the hall. Sticking out of the broken window pane was the ugliest face that anyone in the hall had ever seen. A bushy red eyebrow covered the small left eye. The other eye was completely hidden by a huge wart. The teeth were broken and uneven, with many gaps in between. One tooth hung over the bottom lip, like an elephant's tusk. The mouth looked like a horseshoe. The nose was beyond words.

The crowd spoke with one voice. It chose the owner of this face as the prince of fools. With that the chapel doors opened, and the new prince stepped into the hall. The crowd gasped. The new prince hadn't just been making faces. He really looked like that! And there was more! The rest of his body was just as ugly as his face. His back was hunched. His hands were huge. His feet were broad. One leg was shorter than the other.

The man was Quasimodo. He was the person who rang the bells at Notre Dame Cathedral. Many

people had heard of him. Some were afraid of him. But before today, only a few had ever had a good look at him. Quasimodo spent most of his time in the bell tower of Notre Dame. How he came to be in the great hall, no one knew.

Just then Jacques Coppenole went up to the winner. He patted Quasimodo on the shoulder and said, "You're wonderful! You're a perfect prince of fools!"

But Quasimodo made no answer.

An old woman said, "He's deaf. He became deaf from ringing the bells."

Coppenole laughed and said, "That's even better.

Come, let's fix him up for the parade!"

Quasimodo sat silently. The crowd placed a fake crown on his head and draped him in mock robes. Then they put him in a large, shallow wooden box called a barrow. A dozen men lifted the barrow on their shoulders and paraded Quasimodo around the great hall. Then they danced into the streets of Paris with the new prince of fools.

Quickly the hall emptied. The last to leave was poor Gringoire. As he left, he muttered between his teeth, "These stupid Parisians! They come to see a play, but they don't watch it. Instead, they crown a prince of fools. What a pack of donkeys and clowns!"

2 Esmeralda

In January, night fell early. The streets were already dark when Gringoire left the Palace of Justice. So, too, were his thoughts. He had hoped to earn money from his play, but the play had failed. Now his pockets were empty. He had nowhere to sleep and nothing to eat. He roamed the streets for hours, wondering what to do. At last he came to the banks of the river Seine, where a horrible thought crossed his mind.

"Maybe I should drown myself," he said aloud. But how cold the water would be! He thought instead of warm fires. Then he remembered that there was always a huge bonfire at the Feast of Fools. It burned in the Greve, a large public square on the Seine. Gringoire hurried there. He might be poor and homeless, but at least there he could stay warm. Maybe he could even find some food.

The Greve was a large square. It was bordered on one side by docks. On the other three sides were tall and narrow houses. In the middle of the square, a pillory and a gallows stood side by side. These two grim objects were used to punish people who had broken the law. And in those days, the law was very cruel. Many innocent people were punished. Some were tied to the pillory and whipped. Others were hanged from the gallows.

During the day, these two objects cast a long shadow of pain and death across the Greve. Tonight, however, the square was filled with the light of a merry bonfire. A large crowd had gathered to feel the warmth.

Next to the blazing fire, a young girl danced across a Persian rug, playing a tambourine. Her name was Esmeralda. The crowd watched her with pleasure. Her dancing was almost like magic.

When Gringoire entered the Greve, he was overcome by the sight of Esmeralda. She was brown and slender. Her tiny feet fit easily into her dainty shoes. She danced, she turned, she twirled. And every time she turned, her black eyes seemed to flash with lightning.

She wore a golden vest and skirts of many colors. She had bare shoulders and shapely legs. Her hair was black . . . her eyes were flames.

Gringoire gazed at the girl in wonder. "She must be a goddess," he thought. And then he looked more closely. She was a gypsy. "No matter," he thought. Gringoire was under her spell.

So, too, was another man in the crowd. He was a priest. Although he was only 35 years old, he was already bald. Wrinkles crossed his forehead, but his

eyes gleamed with greed. He kept them fixed on the gypsy. From time to time, he sighed.

The young girl stopped at last. The people clapped loudly. Then the girl said, "Djali! It's your turn now."

A little white goat with gilded horns and hoofs came forward. Esmeralda laid the tambourine at her feet.

"Djali, what time of day is it?" she asked.

Djali lifted her hoof and tapped the tambourine seven times. At that instant the big clock on the Greve struck seven. The crowd was amazed.

"She is a witch," said the bald man. His voice was mean.

"Ah," said Esmeralda. "It is that ugly man again!" She turned away from him. She held out her tambourine to another part of the crowd. People threw pennies and silver coins into the little drum. Then Esmeralda held the drum in front of Gringoire. He reached into his pockets and found nothing. She kept standing before him. She looked at him with her big eyes. She waited. Gringoire didn't know what to do.

A sudden noise saved him. The wild Feast of Fools parade suddenly burst upon the square from a side street. First came the beggars. They were dressed in rags and tatters. Then came the thieves. Some were missing legs; others had no arms. Among them rode the king of thieves in a small cart drawn by two big dogs. After the thieves came the gamblers, and so on.

The parade was made up of people who lived on the streets of Paris. They were called vagrants. There were thousands of them. This was their night. And tonight they were ruled by the prince of fools. He rode in the middle of the parade. A dozen men carried him on his royal barrow.

Quasimodo liked being their prince. Because he was deaf, he could not hear the wild cheers of his ragged subjects. Still he felt like a real prince. His ugly, twisted face seemed touched by joy.

The next moment, that joy turned to terror. The bald priest rushed up to Quasimodo and pulled the mock robes off him. The hunchback leapt from the barrow. He made one jump toward the bald priest and fell to his knees.

"Look!" exclaimed Gringoire. "It's Don Claude Frollo, the archdeacon of Notre Dame!"

Gringoire had known Frollo for a long time. He was surprised to see the priest in the Greve. But today was a day of surprises.

Frollo was not only an archdeacon. He was also Quasimodo's master. He had found the hunchback many years before and had raised him inside the church. But the priest treated Quasimodo more like a slave than a son. He kept him hidden away in the bell tower of Notre Dame Cathedral.

Quasimodo kneeled low before Don Frollo, who ripped the fake crown off the hunchback's head. The two of them began to signal to each other with their hands. Quasimodo rose, and the strange pair began to make their way out of the square.

Some of the vagrants tried to follow. But Quasimodo growled at them like a wild beast. They shrank away in fear. In an instant the bald priest and the hunchback had vanished down a dark, narrow street.

Gringoire watched them go. But his mind quickly turned to other matters. He saw that Esmeralda was also leaving the square. Without knowing quite why, he decided to follow her. Maybe following a pretty woman would take his mind off his troubles. Maybe she could help him find food and shelter.

Gringoire followed the gypsy into streets he had never walked before. Soon she entered a maze of lanes and cross-streets and blind alleys. Their path was like a ball of thread tangled by a kitten. And yet Esmeralda never stopped. She knew exactly where she was going. Her feet seemed to move faster and faster.

By this time, the streets were nearly empty. Gringoire tried to walk quietly, but at last Esmeralda heard his footsteps. She turned around and glanced at him. To Gringoire, that glance seemed full of scorn. He hung his head. He began counting the paving stones under his feet.

When Gringoire next looked up, the gypsy had vanished around a turn in the street. Suddenly, he heard her scream loudly. He ran past the turn in the street. There she was, struggling in the arms of two men.

Gringoire rushed forward. One of the men turned toward him. It was Quasimodo. With one arm he was holding Esmeralda. With the other he picked up Gringoire and flung the poor poet far down the street.

"Help! Murder!" shouted Esmeralda. Quasimodo and the second man hurried away with her.

Just then a horseman stepped out in front of them. He yelled, "Halt, you wretches! Let that woman go!"

The horseman was a captain of the king's archers. He was armed from head to foot. He held a sword in his hand. He tore the gypsy from Quasimodo's arms and swung her into his saddle. Before the hunchback could take her back, 15 archers appeared, swords in hand.

Quasimodo was surrounded. He roared. He foamed at the mouth. He bit. If it had been daylight, his face might have scared the archers. But at night he could not use his most powerful weapon— his ugliness.

The archers finally seized Quasimodo. During the struggle, however, the second man disappeared.

Esmeralda stared straight at the captain. She was charmed by his beauty. In her sweet voice, she asked, "What is your name?"

"Captain Phoebus, at your service, my pretty maid!" came the answer.

"Thank you," she said.

And while Captain Phoebus twirled his mustache, the gypsy slipped from his horse as quick as lightning and fled. "By the pope's head!" said the captain. "I should have held on to that beauty!"

One of his men said, "The bird has flown, but the bat remains."

3 The Court of Miracles

Gringoire still lay facedown in the dark street. He was weak and dizzy from his fall. As he came back to life, he heard a crowd of boys running toward him. Their wooden shoes clattered on the paving stones. They dragged a large sack after them.

"Let's make a bonfire with the sack!" one of them yelled. The other boys agreed at once. Then they threw the sack on top of Gringoire, whom they had not seen. One of them walked up with a bit of flaming straw.

Gringoire's strength returned with amazing speed. He rose to his feet. Then he hurled the sack back at the boys and fled.

"It's a ghost!" screamed the boys. And they flew the other way.

Gringoire ran as fast as his legs could carry him. He didn't even think of where he was going. He soon became hopelessly lost in the maze of dark streets. At last he slowed to a walk and looked around. At the end of a long, narrow lane he could see the glow of a bright fire.

Walking toward the fire, Gringoire noticed strange shapes moving slowly down the street. He looked at

17

them more closely. They were all crippled. One was a man who seemed to have only one arm and one leg. Another had no legs at all. A third was blind.

"Bread!" they begged. "Bread for the lame!"

"I have none," answered Gringoire. And he hurried away. To his surprise, all three cripples hurried after him. He turned and saw that they were not cripples at all. They were thieves! They chased him into a vast, muddy square that was filled with people.

"Where am I?" asked the terrified Gringoire.

"In the Court of Miracles!" came the answer. Gringoire shuddered. So this was the fearful court, which not even the police dared to enter! In this spot the vagrants of Paris gathered each night to feast and make merry. They were all here: beggars, thieves, tramps, and robbers.

"Take him to the king!" the vagrants shouted. "To the king!"

The three thieves grabbed Gringoire. They dragged him toward the fire. Men, women, and children of all shapes and sizes were gathered round the blaze. They were eating, drinking, laughing, and singing.

Near the fire, a beggar sat on the top of a barrel. He was the king of the Court of Miracles. The barrel was his throne. In his hand he held a whip. The thieves dumped Gringoire at his feet.

"Who is this rascal?" asked the king.

The words seemed to stick in Gringoire's throat. He said, "Oh, great king, I . . . I am the author . . . "

"Enough!" cried the king. "You must be hanged. Quite a simple matter. You look like an honest citizen. We treat honest citizens in the same way they treat us: we hang them."

A chill ran down Gringoire's spine. "But I am a poet," he said. "And poets are not honest citizens!"

The king thought for a minute. "If that is so, then you do have one hope. If you agree to join our band, you will not be hanged."

"I agree with all my heart."

"Good," answered the king. "But first you must pass a test. You must fumble the snot."

At these words, several thieves ran to a dark corner of the court. They returned with a wooden gallows. A scarecrow hung from the gallows by the neck. He was dressed in red and covered with bells. Underneath the hanging scarecrow, the thieves placed a rickety old footstool.

The king spoke to Gringoire. He said, "First you will climb up on that footstool. Then you will wrap your right foot around your left leg and stand tiptoe on your left foot. Then you will reach into the scarecrow's pockets and pull out a purse. If you can do all that without ringing the scarecrow's bells, you can join our gang. We call it fumbling the snot."

Gringoire did as he was told. He climbed up on

the footstool. He stood tiptoe on his left foot. He reached for the scarecrow—and fell to the ground. As he fell, he hit the scarecrow. The bells began ringing wildly.

The king spoke to the thieves. "Take down the scarecrow. Put the poet in his place. He has failed the test."

Within seconds Gringoire was on the footstool again. This time the rope was around his neck.

"One moment," said the king. "I almost forgot! We never hang a man without first asking if a woman will marry him."

Gringoire breathed again.

"Ladies!" cried the king to the crowd. "Will any of you marry this rascal?"

Three women stepped forward. The first asked if he had any money.

"None," came the reply.

"Be hanged then!" she said. She turned her back on him.

The second looked at his clothes. She found them too old. The third looked at his arms. She found them too thin.

The king asked, "Will no one take this man? Going, going . . ."

At that instant a shout rose from the vagrants. "Esmeralda! Esmeralda!"

The gypsy girl and her goat, Djali, walked toward the king and Gringoire. Thieves, beggars, and tramps stood aside to let her pass. Every face seemed to brighten at her glance.

"Are you going to hang this man?" she asked the king.

"Yes," he replied. "Unless you'll take him for your husband."

"I'll take him," she said.

Gringoire was let down from the stool. He stood next to Esmeralda. The king put his hands on their heads. He spoke to each in turn.

He said, "Brother, she is your wife. Sister, he is your husband. Go!"

A few moments later, Gringoire found himself in a small, warm room. He was alone with Esmeralda and her goat. Suddenly he wondered if he was living in a fairy tale. In one day he had gone from the edge of death to the heights of joy. And before him stood the beautiful angel who had saved his life.

"She must love me madly," thought Gringoire. With this idea in mind, he approached Esmeralda with open arms.

"What do you want?" she asked, staring at him.

"Oh, come now! Am I not yours, sweet friend? Are you not mine?" And he grabbed her around the waist.

Her vest slipped through his hands like a snake's skin. She leapt to the other side of the room, stooped down, and rose with a tiny dagger in her hands. The goat stood in front of her. It lowered its two sharp horns.

"You're a bold one!" she hissed.

"Forgive me," said Gringoire with a smile. "But why did you marry me, then?"

"Was I to let them hang you?"

"Then you married me only to save my life?"

"What else would you have had me do?"

Gringoire bit his lip. So she didn't love him after all. "No matter," he thought. At least she could give him food and a place to sleep. To tell the truth, Gringoire valued food and sleep more than love.

He said, "I will not come near you again. But please give me some supper."

The gypsy laughed. She put away her knife. A moment later, bread, bacon, apples, and beer were on the table. Gringoire ate greedily.

"Then you don't want me as a husband or a lover?" he asked at last.

"No," Esmeralda said.

"As a friend?" Gringoire asked.

"Perhaps," she answered.

Gringoire thought about this answer. Then all at once he remembered how Quasimodo had tried to grab Esmeralda. "But how did you escape the hunchback?" he asked.

Esmeralda said nothing. She shivered. Then she smiled sweetly.

"Do you know why he followed you?" Gringoire went on.

"No, I don't. But didn't you follow me as well?" she asked. "Why did you do that?"

"I have forgotten," answered the poet.

The two of them sat silently for some time. Gringoire noticed that Esmeralda wore a necklace made of beads. From this necklace hung a green bag. It had a bit of green glass on the outside, like an emerald.

"Is that why they call you Esmeralda?" he asked. And he reached for the little green bag.

She drew away from his hand. "Don't touch the necklace! You'll break the charm," she said.

With that the two fell silent once more. At last Esmeralda spoke again.

"Do you know what *Phoebus* means?" she asked.

"It's the name of the Roman god of the sun," said Gringoire.

"A god!" she murmured. Her voice was filled with love.

At that moment one of her bracelets fell to the ground. Gringoire bent down to pick it up. When he rose, the girl and the goat had disappeared. He heard a bolt slide across her bedroom door.

"At least I hope she has left me a bed!" thought the poet.

Gringoire walked around the room. There was nothing fit to sleep on except a long wooden chest with a bumpy lid. He made himself as comfortable as he could. Then he closed his eyes and quickly fell fast asleep.

4 A Tear for a Drop of Water

On the morning of January 7th, 1482, Judge Robert d'Estouteville woke in a very bad mood. It was the day after the Feast of Fools. His courtroom would be busy all day long. The police had made many arrests the day before. Now it was his job to sentence the criminals.

By the time the judge had reached his courtroom, it was already filled with people. He walked in through a back door. Then he sat down in his large oak armchair behind a wooden table.

Before the table stood his first case. It was Quasimodo. He was tied with rope and well guarded. A squad of police surrounded him. Behind them was a railing. Behind the railing stood the crowd.

The judge spoke sharply to the hunchback: "What brings you here, you ugly thing?"

The deaf hunchback thought that the judge had asked his name. "Quasimodo," he answered. His voice was low and hoarse.

The answer had so little to do with the question that the crowd laughed. The judge turned red with rage. He cried out, "Do you mock me, you oaf?"

"Bell ringer of Notre Dame," said Quasimodo.

"Bell ringer, indeed! I'll have the whips ring on your back through all the streets of Paris! Do you hear me, you rascal?"

"If you want to know my age, I am almost 20," Quasimodo said.

This was too much. The judge could bear it no longer. He told the police, "Take him to the pillory in the Greve. Beat him well. Let him turn for two hours. He shall pay for his rudeness!"

Later that day, four mounted police took their places at the four corners of the pillory. A large, noisy crowd gathered. They hoped to see a good whipping. The noise of the crowd reached every corner of the square.

Near one of these corners was a narrow window crossed by two iron bars. The window was the only opening to a tiny cell built against the wall of an old house. People called the cell the rat hole. But it was the home, not of rats, but of a lonely old woman.

The woman's name was Sister Gudule. She was a nun. She had lived in the rat hole for many years. Her hair hung down to the ground. So did her sack-like dress. On this cold day, she seemed to have been turned to stone. She was like a statue. Her hands were clasped together as she sat and stared at a corner of her cell.

In that corner sat a tiny pink satin shoe. It was the shoe of her baby daughter. Sixteen years ago Gudule had been an unwed mother. The baby girl was all that she had in the world. Then gypsies stole her baby from her. Gudule spent years looking for the stolen child, but she was nowhere to be found.

Eventually Gudule moved into the rat hole. Here she prayed for the child's life even as her own life faded away. She grew to hate the sight of gypsies. Whenever gypsies entered the Greve, Gudule cursed them loudly.

No one in the crowd was looking at the rat hole just now. All eyes were fixed on the police officers and the pillory. The pillary was a hollow cube of stone about ten feet high. On top of the cube was a flat wheel made of oak. A shaft ran from the wheel into the cube. A machine inside the cube made the shaft turn the wheel around and around.

At last the police brought Quasimodo into the square. They tied him to the pillory wheel with straps and ropes. Meanwhile the crowd laughed and hooted. This was the prince of fools! Just last night he had ruled over all of Paris. Yet today he was pilloried in the Greve. It was too funny for words.

Suddenly a trumpet sounded. A man with a whip climbed up to the top of the cube and stood next to the wheel. He placed a black hourglass filled with red sand on a corner of the pillory. The sand began to fall from the top to the bottom of the glass. It showed that Quasimodo's first hour had just begun.

The man with the whip stamped his foot. The wheel began to turn. When Quasimodo's back faced him, the man lashed out with his whip. The lashes hissed through the air like snakes. Then they smashed into the poor hunchback's bare shoulders.

Quasimodo writhed in pain. A second blow followed the first. Then a third, then a fourth, and on and on. The wheel kept turning; the blows kept coming.

Soon the blood spurted. It streamed across the hunchback's shoulders. The whip sprinkled it in drops across the crowd.

At first Quasimodo tried to break free. He

struggled with all his might. But the straps and ropes held firm. The more he struggled, the more they cut into his flesh.

He fell back at last. He closed his one good eye. Then he moved no more. Nothing could make him move. The blood kept flowing, and the blows kept falling. But Quasimodo stayed as still as a statue.

Finally the last bits of sand fell to the bottom of the hourglass. The whip stopped. The wheel stopped. Quasimodo's eye opened once again.

The whipping was over. Two men climbed up the pillory. They washed Quasimodo's bleeding shoulders. Then they threw a piece of yellow cotton cloth over his back.

But all was not over for Quasimodo. He still had to spend one more hour in the pillory. For this reason, the men turned the hourglass back over before climbing down.

Now it was the crowd's turn to torture the hunchback. First they cursed and laughed at him. Then they threw stones. He put up with this for a time. But at last he could stand it no more. He tried once again to break free of the ropes that held him. He made the wheel creak, but that was all. The crowd laughed even more loudly than before.

Bit by bit, rage, hate, and sadness clouded the face of Quasimodo. Then, at one point, a mule passed through the crowd. A priest was riding on its back. As soon as Quasimodo saw the priest, his face softened. The dark cloud gave way to a strange smile. It was full of sweetness. Just then, however, the priest cast down his eyes. He seemed to be afraid of something. He turned around quickly and rode out of the square. It was the bald archdeacon of Notre Dame, Don Claude Frollo.

Time passed slowly. The cloud on Quasimodo's face grew darker than ever. He had been on the pillory for at least an hour and a half. Suddenly he began to speak. His voice sounded like the bark of a dog. "Water!" he cried out.

Everyone laughed.

One young man shouted, "Drink this, you deaf monster!" He picked up a sponge that had been dragged through the gutter. Then he threw it right in the hunchback's face. The crowd laughed again.

"Water!" repeated the hunchback.

With that the crowd parted, and Esmeralda stepped out. Quasimodo recognized the gypsy girl he had tried to carry off the night before. He shook with fear. He thought she had come to take her turn at him with the rest.

Without a word, she climbed up the pillory. Fearing the worst, the hunchback tried to twist out of her way. But it was no use. Suddenly, she reached into her gown and pulled out a flask of water. She raised it gently to his parched lips.

A great tear trickled from his dry and burning eye. It rolled down his twisted, ugly face. It was the first tear that Quasimodo had ever shed.

He drank long and well. When he was done, the hunchback put out his lips as if to kiss the fair hand that had helped him. But Esmeralda drew back in fear. The poor man gave her a look of great sadness.

Even the crowd was touched by the sight. A minute ago they had been hurling rocks. Now they began to weep.

At this instant a loud noise came from the rat hole, the cell in the corner of the Greve. Sister Gudule had seen the gypsy girl upon the pillory. She yelled at her in a voice heard around the square. "My curse on you, you foul gypsy!" she shouted. "May you be cursed forever!"

The crowd fell silent. Esmeralda turned pale. She climbed down from the pillory. But the voice still followed her.

"Come down, come down, you gypsy thief! You'll hang from the gallows soon enough!" The people whispered among themselves as Esmeralda left the square. No one dared to raise a voice against Sister Gudule. She prayed day and night, and the people were in awe of her.

Finally the two hours were over. The police untied Quasimodo. With that the crowd went on its way.

5 P-H-O-E-B-U-S

Notre Dame Cathedral has two towers: the north tower and the south tower. Quasimodo always loved to ring the bells in the north tower. He rang them for weddings, for holidays, for any days. It seemed as though the bells of the old church were always ringing and filled with joy. But that was before Quasimodo was pilloried.

Now that joy was gone. The bells seemed to ring only for funerals. Everyone wondered what had happened to Quasimodo. Had the pillory made him lose his love for the bells? Or did the bells have a new rival in Quasimodo's heart? No one knew.

Then spring came. Quasimodo's love for the bells finally returned during a holiday at the end of March. It was a clear, warm day. He climbed the north tower and once again set the bells ringing. He was happy again. He had forgotten everything. He ran from one rope to another. He pulled the ropes and watched the bells swing back and forth.

He cried, "Go on! Go on, you bells! Pour your music into the square! Today is a holiday. That's good! The sun shines bright. The people want to hear the bells. Make them all as deaf as I am!"

On clear days such as this there is one hour when the front of Notre Dame cathedral is especially beautiful. This is the hour when the setting sun faces the cathedral. The sun's rays climb the face of the church and light up its many statues. Meanwhile, the great rose window above the doors seems to burst into flames of light. It was now just that hour.

As he worked, Quasimodo looked down at the square far below him. Before long he saw a young girl spreading a carpet on the ground. She had a little goat and a tambourine.

Quasimodo instantly stopped ringing the bells and ran to a window. He stared down at the square. Meanwhile, the people below wondered what had happened to the bells. Why had they stopped so suddenly?

Across the square from the mighty cathedral, a group of lovely young girls sat on the stone balcony of a handsome house. They were wearing pearls, silks, and velvets. It was clear that they were daughters of the rich. Their soft white hands had never seen a day of hard work.

The stone balcony opened into a well-furnished room where other girls were sitting. Among them was Fleur-de-Lys, who lived in the house with her mother, who was a widow. This woman sat in a thick red-velvet armchair. Next to her stood

Captain Phoebus, in full uniform.

The girls were weaving a large tapestry, in which there was a picture of Neptune, the Roman god of the sea, in his underwater palace. When it was completed, this tapestry would be hung on the wall of a church.

Captain Phoebus was engaged to be married to Fleur-de-Lys. It was clear from the bored look on his face that he was not in love. The girl was rich, however, and captains rarely marry poor girls.

The widow had not noticed how bored the captain was. Instead, she pulled his sleeve and whispered secretly to him.

"Have you ever seen a more beautiful face than my daughter's?" she asked. "Aren't her hands clever? Isn't her neck perfect? How I envy you! How lucky you are to be marrying her!"

"Of course," he answered. But his mind was on other things.

The widow gave him a little push. "Why don't you talk to her? Say something. There's no need to be shy."

Now, the captain was far from shy. In fact, he was well known in the local taverns. He could be very bold indeed. But in this room, with these ladies, he was only bored.

Eventually Captain Phoebus walked over to Fleur-de-Lys and tried to make small talk. The widow smiled. She did not know that the future husband and wife had little to say to each other.

Just then, one of the girls on the balcony cried out, "Oh, look at that dear dancing girl down there on the square! She's playing a tambourine!"

The sound of the tambourine was heard by all.

"It's a gypsy girl," said Fleur-de-Lys. Then she turned toward the square.

"Let's see! Let's see!" cried the girls. And they all ran to the edge of the balcony. Fleur-de-Lys followed them slowly. The captain, meanwhile, returned to the far end of the room.

Fleur-de-Lys came back inside. "Captain," she said, "didn't you tell us about a little gypsy girl? You said you rescued her from a dozen robbers about two months ago."

"I think I did," came the answer.

"Come and see if you know her," said Fleur-de-Lys.

Captain Phoebus walked to the balcony. He looked at the dancing gypsy. Then he said, "Yes, it is she. I know her by her goat."

"So you do know the little gypsy! Please ask her to come up," begged Fleur-de-Lys. "We would like to see her."

"Oh, yes!" cried all the girls. And they clapped their hands.

"Whatever you want, my dears," Phoebus answered. "She has probably forgotten me. I don't

even know her name. Still, if you like, I will try."

The captain leaned over the balcony railing. Then he called out, "Little one!"

The gypsy turned her eyes toward Phoebus, stopping short. The captain called her again. He said, "Little one! Please come up."

Esmeralda looked at him once more. She blushed as if her cheeks were on fire. Then she put her tambourine under her arm, and she and Djali moved toward the house. A moment later, they stood in the upstairs room.

Esmeralda's beauty was so great that all of the rich young ladies felt a hint of envy.

Phoebus said, "My pretty child, I don't know if you remember me, but . . . "

The little gypsy interrupted him with a smile. "Oh, yes!" She said.

"She has a good memory," said Fleur-de-Lys.

"You escaped very quickly," said Phoebus. "Did I frighten you?"

"Oh, no!" said Esmeralda.

The gypsy's tone of voice wounded Fleur-de-Lys. The bride-to-be looked quickly from the smiling captain to the lovely gypsy. Her heart filled with pain and anger. That anger grew when the captain turned to the group and said, "Isn't she a lovely girl?"

"Very badly dressed," said Fleur-de-Lys, in a low

voice. This remark encouraged the other girls. They could find no fault with Esmeralda's beauty, so they, too, attacked her clothes. They took turns making fun of her skirts, her belt, and her vest.

Meanwhile, the youngest girl had noticed a leather bag hanging from the goat's neck. She was curious to know what was inside. So she used a piece of candy to lure Djali into a corner of the room. She removed the bag from the goat's neck and opened it. Inside were all the letters of the alphabet, cut out of wood. The girl poured the letters on the floor.

Djali set right to work. She had learned a new trick. Using her hoofs, she arranged the letters into a word. The girl looked down at the word. Then she cried out, "Fleur-de-Lys! Come and see what the goat has done!"

Everyone hurried over. The letters on the floor spelled out P-H-O-E-B-U-S.

"Why, that's the captain's name!" whispered the girls.

"What a good memory you have!" said Fleur-de-Lys, bursting into sobs. She hid her face in her lovely hands and stammered out, "Oh, she is a witch!" Then she fainted.

"My daughter! My daughter!" screamed the widow. "Begone, you devilish gypsy!"

Esmeralda picked up the letters in a flash. She

went out one door as the girls carried Fleur-de-Lys through another.

Captain Phoebus, left alone, paused for a moment between the two doors. Then he followed the gypsy.

While all of this was taking place, two other characters were meeting on the other side of the square. One was the archdeacon Frollo. The other was Pierre Gringoire.

As usual, Frollo had climbed up the north tower of Notre Dame an hour before sunset. All of Paris lay beneath his feet. People flowed through its maze of streets. The Seine wound its way from one end of the city to the other. But Frollo was not looking at the streets or at the river. His gaze was fixed on the dancing Esmeralda.

Another person kept entering Frollo's view. This was a tall, thin man dressed in a red and yellow coat. He seemed to be the gypsy's helper.

Frollo muttered, "Who is that man? She has always been alone until now."

Then he ran down the winding stairs of the tower. As he did so, he passed Quasimodo. The hunchback was staring out at the square through a window. He did not hear his master hurrying by.

Frollo reached the square at last. But Esmeralda had disappeared into the house of Fleur-de-Lys. The unknown man in the red and yellow coat was still there. It was Pierre Gringoire.

The priest knew the poet, but he had not seen him for a long time. Now he said, "Why, it's you! What are you doing here?"

Before Gringoire could answer, Frollo took him inside the dark and empty cathedral. There Gringoire explained how he had come to be Esmeralda's husband.

Frollo's eyes blazed with anger. "How could you have laid your hands on that girl?" he cried.

Gringoire answered, "I haven't. She won't let me touch her. She is an orphan. Around her neck she wears a kind of charm in a green bag. She believes that the charm will help her find her parents. But if she sleeps with a man, the charm will lose its power."

"Then you are husband and wife in name only?" asked the priest.

"Yes," Gringoire answered. "I help her collect money from the crowds who watch her dance. In return, she feeds me and lets me sleep in her kitchen. But that is all. We are more like brother and sister than man and wife."

"And does the goat live with you as well?" asked the priest.

"Djali? Of course," Gringoire replied. "That goat is amazing. Esmeralda has taught her to spell the word *Phoebus* with wooden letters."

"Phoebus?" the priest asked. "And who might that be?"

"Why, the Roman god of the sun, of course," Gringoire said. "He is the only Phoebus I know of. I believe that gypsies worship him."

A black cloud seemed to pass over Frollo's face. "Phoebus!" he cried. Then he suddenly turned and walked away. He faded into the darkness of the cathedral.

6 The Ghostly Monk

The famous tavern known as the Apple of Eve was a large, low room at street level. It had tables everywhere and shining jugs hanging on the walls. It was always filled with drinkers, girls, and wine jugs.

The sign of the tavern hung over the door. It was the picture of a woman painted on a piece of iron. It swung in the wind and rusted in the rain.

Night was falling. The streets of Paris were dark. The tavern, full of glowing candles, lit up a corner of the city. The noise of clinking glasses and loud arguments escaped through the tavern's broken window panes.

Outside the tavern, a man was marching back and forth like a guard. His coat was pulled up to his nose. His hat was pulled down to his eyes. From time to time he stopped in front of the window. Here he listened, looked, and stamped his feet.

At last the tavern door opened. The waiting man stepped back into the shadows. Two drunks came out. One was Captain Phoebus.

"Thunder and guns!" the captain said. "It's time for my date with the gypsy."

His companion staggered back and forth. He said,

"The gypsy? I think the stars are on fire."

Phoebus answered, "Jehan, my friend, you are drunk. By the way, do you have any money left?"

"Money? Honey? Funny?" asked his friend.

"Jehan, friend Jehan! I'm taking her to that inn on Saint Michael's Bridge. I'll need money to pay for the room. Don't you have any more?"

"The sea, so deep and wide, is frozen at the tide."

"You fool!" cried Phoebus. And he pushed his friend away. The drunken Jehan fell down. He closed his eyes and began snoring. He did not have a penny on him.

The captain hurried away. He soon discovered that someone was following him. It was the man from outside the tavern. Phoebus looked over his shoulder. He saw a kind of shadow creeping behind him along the walls. He stopped; it stopped. He walked on again; the shadow also walked on.

Phoebus stopped again on a dark street. The shadow came close, stopped, and then stood as still as a statue. Phoebus was brave, but this walking statue made his blood stand still. He remembered hearing stories about a ghostly monk who prowled the streets of Paris at night.

Phoebus called out, "Sir, if you are a robber, you've got the wrong man. I don't have a penny on me." Just then the shadow's hand gripped the captain's arm tightly. Then the shadow spoke.

"Captain Phoebus!" it called.

"What the devil! How do you know my name?"

"I know many things. I know that you have an important appointment this evening."

"Yes," answered the captain.

"You are going to take the gypsy girl Esmeralda to the inn on Saint Michael's Bridge. Is that not so?"

"Yes, but I have no money to pay for the room."

"Here is some money." Then the man slipped a coin into the captain's hand.

Phoebus shouted, "By God! You're a good fellow!"

The man answered, "It's yours on one condition. Prove to me that you're telling the truth. Hide me in a corner of the room at the inn. I want to see if this woman is really Esmeralda."

Phoebus answered, "With all my heart! We will take the room with the closet. They call it Saint Martha's room. You can look on from there."

"Come on, then!" said the man.

They walked quickly. In a few minutes the sound of the river told them that they stood on Saint Michael's Bridge. At that time, the bridge was covered with houses.

Phoebus said, "I'll hide you first. Then I'll go fetch the gypsy."

He knocked loudly on a low door. An old woman opened it. She was hunched over and dressed in rags. Phoebus handed her the coin. He said, "Give us Saint Martha's room."

The old woman knew the captain well. She took a lamp and led the men upstairs. When they entered the room, Phoebus opened the closet door for the man in the cloak. The captain tried in vain to see the man's face, but he kept it hidden.

"Go in there. I'll be right back," said the captain.

The man obeyed without a word. Phoebus shut the door, and the light disappeared.

The man in the closet was Claude Frollo. His head was burning hot. He groped around in the dark for quite some time. Then he felt around with his hands and found a bit of broken glass. He pressed the glass against his forehead. Its coolness refreshed him.

Frollo waited in the closet for 15 minutes. It felt like a hundred years. At last he heard someone on the stairs. The door to the room opened, and a light appeared.

There was a large hole in the closet door. Frollo glued his face against the hole. He could see everything that happened in the room. First came the old woman with the lamp. Then came Phoebus, twirling his mustache. Last came the lovely Esmeralda, followed by her goat.

The old woman set the lamp on a chest and left the room. Frollo could see a bed behind the chest. Next to the bed was a window. One could hear the river flowing by from the window.

The young girl was blushing, trembling, and confused. She dared not raise her eyes to the captain's happy face.

The gypsy said, "Oh, do not hate me, my lord Phoebus. I feel that I am doing something very wrong."

"Hate you, my dear child? But why?" replied the captain.

"Because I am breaking a sacred vow. Now I shall never find my parents! The charm will lose its power. But what does that matter? Why should I need a father or a mother now?"

"What on earth are you talking about?" asked Phoebus.

Esmeralda was silent for a moment. Then a tear fell from her eyes and a sigh from her lips. "Oh, my lord, I love you!" she said.

"You love me!" he said. And he threw his arm around her waist. This was the chance he had been waiting for.

The gypsy gave him a few little taps on the lips with her pretty hand. She asked him, "Do you love me? I want you to tell me if you love me."

The captain let go of her waist. Then he knelt before her. "Do I love you, angel of my life? My body, my soul, my blood, are yours. I am all yours—all yours. I love you. I have never loved anyone but you."

The captain had made this speech to others so often that he didn't make a single mistake. He gave it in one breath.

The gypsy answered, "Oh, at such a moment one might well wish to die."

"To die? But it is just the time to live!" exclaimed Phoebus.

Esmeralda made no answer. Her silence made the captain feel bold. He began to untie her scarf. The girl let Phoebus have his way. She did not seem to be aware of what he was doing. His eyes gleamed.

All at once Phoebus pulled off the scarf. Esmeralda sprang up with a start. She glanced at her bare shoulders. Then she crossed her arms across her chest.

Now that the scarf was off, Phoebus could see the strange green bag that hung from Esmeralda's neck. "What is this?" he asked, drawing closer.

She answered, "Do not touch it! It will help me find my family! Oh, leave me, Phoebus! Mother, where are you? Help me now! Phoebus, give me back my scarf!"

The captain drew back from her. Then he said in a cold tone, "Oh, I see that you do not love me!"

"I not love you, my Phoebus? How can you say so? Oh, come! Take me, take everything! Do with me what you will; I am yours."

As she said this, she sat down next to the captain.

Then she flung her arms around his neck. She gazed up at his face through her tears with a lovely smile. The captain pressed his burning lips to her bare shoulders. The young girl fixed her eyes on the ceiling. She trembled at the captain's kiss.

All at once Esmeralda saw a face above Phoebus's head. Beside the face was a hand that held a dagger. Phoebus could not see the face. It was Frollo the priest. The girl was frozen, mute. She could not even utter a cry.

Suddenly Esmeralda saw the dagger plunge into Phoebus's back. She heard a yell of pain. Then she fainted. As her eyes closed, she felt a fiery kiss upon her lips.

When Esmeralda came to, the room was full of soldiers. Some of them were carrying the bloody captain out the door. The priest had vanished. The window next to the bed was wide open.

Esmeralda heard a soldier say, "She is a witch who has stabbed a captain."

7 The Palace of Justice

Back in the Court of Miracles, the vagrants were in a terrible state. They had not heard from Esmeralda for more than a month. One night she had disappeared along with her goat. Since then, she had not been seen.

Gringoire missed the gypsy, too. He did not love her, but he depended on her. With both Esmeralda and Djali gone, he had no way of making money. To tell the truth, he missed the goat more than he did the gypsy. If only he had the goat, Gringoire thought, he could start making money again.

One evening Gringoire walked sadly by the Palace of Justice. He noticed a large crowd at the door.

"What's going on?" he asked a young man.

The man answered, "I hear they are trying a woman for murdering a captain. It seems she might be a witch. The archdeacon Frollo is one of the judges."

Gringoire followed the crowd into the great hall. He remembered with pain how his play had failed there just a few months before. Now the hall was dimly lighted with candles. Instead of a stage, the marble table held a platform filled with hooded judges. Some were lords; some were priests. Among the judges was the archdeacon Frollo, his face hidden in the shadows. Above the judges hung a huge cross.

The prisoner sat in front of the platform. Her back was to the crowd. A lawyer stood beside her.

The chief judge said, "Woman, you are accused of murdering Captain Phoebus."

At the sound of this name, the prisoner rose. Gringoire saw that it was Esmeralda.

She cried out, "Phoebus! Where is he? Oh please, before you kill me, tell me if he is still alive!" Her chains rattled as she spoke.

The chief judge answered, "Be silent, woman! He is dying! That is all you need to know."

The wretched girl fell back on her seat. The chief judge went on, "Bring in the other prisoner!"

All eyes turned toward a small door. The goat Djali was brought in. The animal quickly romped over to Esmeralda. Then she curled up at Esmeralda's feet.

The lawyer said, "If it please the judges, we shall examine the goat."

Then the lawyer brought the goat before the judges. He laid the gypsy's tambourine on the floor. Turning to Djali, he asked, "What time is it?"

The goat lifted her hoof and struck the tambourine seven times. Whispers of fear ran through the crowd. The same people who had cheered this trick in the streets were terrified to see it in the Palace of Justice. The goat was clearly the devil.

Next the lawyer took the leather bag off the goat's neck. He poured out the wooden letters. The crowd gasped as the goat spelled P-H-O-E-B-U-S. It was now clear that the gypsy had cast a spell on the goat. It was clear that the gypsy was a horrible witch.

The chief judge said, "Woman, you are a gypsy and a witch. You stabbed and murdered Captain Phoebus with the aid of charms and spells. Do you deny it?"

"I do deny it!" she answered, raising her voice.

"Then how do you explain the crime?"

"I have told you already. I do not know. It was a priest, a priest who had long pursued me!"

The judge said, "The ghostly monk! Another servant of the devil. The two of you joined forces to murder the captain!"

"Oh, my lord, have pity! I am only a poor girl."

"You are a gypsy and a witch!" said the judge.

Esmeralda's heart sank. She sobbed aloud in the dark room. She answered feebly, "Do whatever you want, but please kill me quickly."

The judges gathered together on the dark platform. They nodded their heads. They were in a hurry to finish. Esmeralda seemed to be looking at

them, but her dim eyes saw nothing.

The chief judge spoke at last. He said, "Gypsy girl, we find you guilty of stabbing Captain Phoebus. In the month of May, at the hour of noon, you will be taken in a cart to the door of Notre Dame Cathedral. There you shall hold a wax candle and ask God to forgive you for your sins. Then you shall be taken to the Greve, where you will be hanged on the gallows, along with your goat. May God have mercy on your soul!"

"Oh, it is a bad dream!" she murmured. The guards then came and took her away.

During the period of the Middle Ages, there was almost as much of a building below ground as above ground. The parts under the ground were almost like roots. They branched out under the earth into hallways, stairs, and rooms.

This underground part of the palace was a prison. The deeper one went, the darker and colder the prison became.

Anyone who was locked in one of the cells of this prison said good-bye to light, to air, to life, and to hope. The mountain of stones above the cells was like a huge lock. It shut the prisoners off from the living world. The prisoners left their cells only when it was time for them to go to the gallows.

It was in one of these cells, underneath a trapdoor, that Esmeralda was placed. She was as cold as death. No human voices reached her ears. No daylight entered her eyes. She was cramped and crushed beneath her chains.

Esmeralda had neither slept nor awakened since she had been there. She could not tell sleep from wakefulness, dreams from reality, day from night. She felt nothing, knew nothing, thought nothing. How long had she been there? She did not know.

At last, one day—or one night—she heard the trapdoor opening. She saw a reddish ray of light. The light hurt her eyes so cruelly that she shut them. When she reopened them, a tall man stood before her. He wore a long black gown. She could not see the face beneath the dark hood.

"Who are you?" she asked.

"A priest," he replied. The sound of his voice made her tremble.

"Are you prepared to die?" he went on.

"Oh!" she cried. "Will it be soon?"

"Tomorrow," he said.

Having said this, the priest threw back his hood. She looked at him. It was that evil face that had followed her for so long. It was that evil face that had appeared above the head of Captain Phoebus, next to a dagger.

She cried, "Do your work! Strike the last blow!" And her head sank between her shoulders. She was like a lamb waiting for the butcher's ax.

"Do you look on me with horror?" asked Frollo.

She raised her eyes to him, crying out, "You are the one who hurled me into this prison! You are the one who killed Phoebus! Who are you? What have I done to you? Why do you hate me so much?"

"I love you!" exclaimed the priest.

She stared at him. He had fallen on his knees and was gazing at her face with eyes of fire.

"Do you hear? I love you!" he cried again.

She fell silent, stunned by his words.

The priest spoke at last. "Listen, and you shall know all. Before I met you, books were my whole world. As a priest, I vowed that I would never marry. Whenever thoughts of women entered my mind, I had only to open a book to make them vanish."

"But one day," he went on, "as I was reading, I heard the sound of a tambourine. I looked out on the square. There was the most beautiful girl I had ever seen. She was dancing. She seemed to outshine the sun itself. Alas, it was you! And as I looked more closely, the thought entered my mind that you had come from hell! A beauty such as yours could not have come from this earth."

Here the priest stopped to stare at her face. Then he added, "Your charm began to work on me. Your dance went around and around in my brain. I tried to escape it, but it was impossible. From that day forward, I have been in love! I have followed you everywhere. One night I even tried to carry you off."

"So it was you!" said Esmeralda.

The priest said, "Oh, have pity on me! Oh, to love a woman! Oh, to be a priest! I know that you are in love with a soldier. I know that I have nothing to offer you but a priest's dirty gown! If you come here from hell, I will go there with you. We must escape! I have never felt before how much I love you!"

He seized her by the arm. He was frantic. He tried to drag her away.

Esmeralda fixed her eyes on him. "What has happened to Phoebus?" she asked.

"He is dead!" answered the priest.

"Dead!" she cried. "Then why do you talk to me about living?" She threw herself upon the priest, pushing him away. "Begone, you monster! Leave me to die! Be yours, priest? Never! Nothing shall ever unite us—not even hell! Go!"

The priest staggered backward. Then he stumbled up the stairs that led to the trapdoor. Just before closing the door, he cried, "I tell you, Phoebus is dead!"

Esmeralda fell facedown on the ground. The cell echoed with her sobs.

8   Sanctuary

Phoebus was not dead. Men of his kind are hard to kill. The chief judge was wrong when he told Esmeralda that the captain was dying. So was the archdeacon Frollo when he said that he was dead. In fact, these men knew nothing about where Phoebus was. They did not know what had become of him.

The captain's wound was severe but not fatal. After the stabbing, the soldiers had taken him to a doctor's house. He stayed there for a week, healing quickly. Phoebus did not want to be dragged into the scandal of Esmeralda's trial. If Fleur-de-Lys learned of it, she might not marry him after all. And without her money, his life would be ruined.

Therefore, one fine morning Phoebus slipped away from the doctor's house. His disappearance did not disturb the police. The important thing to them was to hang the gypsy. They could prove that she was guilty, thanks to her goat. Whatever happened to Phoebus was not their concern.

As for Phoebus, he simply rejoined his old company of archers, which had been sent to a farming town not far from Paris. He was happy to be away from Paris and the scandal with the gypsy.

The captain's thoughts soon turned again to Fleur-de-Lys. He could not let her slip through his fingers. Besides, the farming girls had little to offer him. One morning in early May he returned to Fleur-de-Lys's house in Paris. He was sure that the gypsy would have been hanged and forgotten by then.

It was almost noon when Phoebus knocked on his sweetheart's door. He paid no heed to the large crowd gathering in the square behind him. He guessed that they were celebrating a holiday.

Fleur-de-Lys was alone with her mother. The girl's mind was still on the scene with the gypsy. But when she saw the handsome Phoebus in his new uniform, she blushed with pleasure. She herself was more lovely than ever.

The three of them sat in the upstairs room next to the balcony. "Where have you been these last two months, you naughty boy?" asked Fleur-de-Lys.

"I had to rejoin my company of archers," answered the captain. And he named the town where it had been staying.

"But that's not far from here. Why didn't you visit before now?"

The captain tried to change the subject. He stepped to the window. Then he said, "My, what a crowd there is in the square!"

Fleur-de-Lys answered, "Yes. I hear that a witch will appear before Notre Dame at noon today. Then she'll be hanged in the Greve."

"Oh," said Phoebus, thinking nothing of it. Witches were hanged all the time in those days. He crossed the room and stood behind his future wife. Meanwhile, her mother had left the room. Feeling bold, the captain eyed the young woman's bare neck and shoulders.

Fleur-de-Lys blushed. She said, "Heavens! How warm I feel!"

Phoebus answered, "Indeed! The sunlight is pouring through the window. I had better close the curtains."

The girl cried, "No, no! I want air." And she ran to the window like a hunted deer. She opened it and rushed out on the balcony. Phoebus followed her.

The sight that greeted their eyes was strange and painful. A grey and dirty mob filled every inch of the square—except for a small space in front of the cathedral. At that instant, the clock of Notre Dame struck twelve. With that, a cart entered the square from Saint Peter's Road. It was drawn by a strong horse and surrounded by soldiers. In the cart sat a young girl, her hands tied behind her. A small green bag hung from her neck. At her feet was a little goat.

Fleur-de-Lys said, "Why, Phoebus, it's that wicked gypsy girl!"

"What gypsy girl?" said the captain, turning pale.

Fleur-de-Lys eyed him with surprise. She

remembered having heard something about a captain and a witch. She asked, "What's the matter? Do you know something about her?"

"Me? Not at all," Phoebus answered.

The captain tried to return inside. But Fleur-de-Lys forced him to remain. Luckily for him, Esmeralda kept her eyes fixed on the bottom of the cart.

The soldiers used whips to part the crowd as the cart rolled across the square. Then the cart stopped in front of the cathedral. The church doors swung open. A line of priests, led by Frollo, slowly walked out. They were chanting a Latin mass for the dead. Frollo wore a silver robe and a black cross.

The soldiers untied Esmeralda's hands and helped her out of the cart. The goat followed. Then they gave her a heavy candle and moved away. She and the goat were now standing in the empty space before the church. Frollo walked into this space. The other priests stayed on the edge.

In a loud voice, he said, "Woman, have you asked God to pardon you?"

Then he bent down to her ear and whispered, "Will you be mine? I can still save you!"

She whispered back, "No! What have you done with my Phoebus?"

"He is dead!" came the answer.

Just then Frollo raised his head and saw Phoebus

standing on the balcony across the square. Frollo staggered. He passed his hand over his eyes. He said to himself, "Phoebus shall never have you! You must die!"

He then raised his hand above the gypsy's head. He cried out, "May God have mercy on your soul!"

The crowd knelt.

"Lord, hear our prayer," said the priests.

"Lord, hear our prayer," echoed the crowd.

"Amen," said the archdeacon.

Frollo then turned around and slowly walked back into the cathedral. The other priests followed him.

The soldiers tied Esmeralda's hands together. As she stood next to the cart, she raised her eyes to heaven, to the sun, to the clouds. Then she cast them down to the crowd and the houses. Just then she gave a shriek—a shriek of joy. There, on the balcony, she had just seen him—her lover, her lord, Phoebus!

"Phoebus!" cried Esmeralda. "Phoebus!"

Then she saw the captain frown. She saw Fleur-de-Lys give him an angry look. She saw them turn around and go back into the house.

"Phoebus!" she cried one last time. And then she fainted.

All this time, a strange person had been watching the scene in the square. He stood on the balcony of Notre Dame. He looked just like one of the stone monsters carved on walls of the cathedral. It was Quasimodo. No one had seen him tie a rope to the railing and let it down to the ground.

The instant that Esmeralda fainted, Quasimodo slid down the rope and rushed toward her. He shoved the soldiers aside and seized the girl in one hand. In a flash, the two were inside the church, along with the goat.

Quasimodo raised Esmeralda above his head and shouted, "Sanctuary!"

"Sanctuary! Sanctuary!" shouted the mob. And they clapped their hands, ten thousand of them. Quasimodo's one eye gleamed with pride.

The soldiers stood frozen in their places. They could do nothing. The church was a place of safety—a sanctuary—for criminals. The soldiers could not enter the church. They would need an order from the king himself to take Esmeralda back. But the king was far away from Paris. He would not be returning for several weeks. The gypsy was safe, at least for now.

Quasimodo held Esmeralda with extreme care. At times he looked as if he dared not touch her, even with his breath. Then all at once, he pressed her close. His eye looked upon her with pity. The crowd cheered, for at that instant Quasimodo was beautiful. He had saved the girl from death. He was a hero.

All at once he dashed farther into the church. A moment later he appeared on the balcony, still holding Esmeralda above his head.

"Sanctuary!" he shouted. The crowd cheered again. Then he dashed back inside and appeared at the bell tower. He wanted to show the whole city of Paris what he had done.

"Sanctuary!" he shouted, in a voice like thunder.

"Sanctuary!" answered the mob. And their shout reached all the way to the Greve, on the other side of the river. The gallows there stood empty. No one would hang from the gallows on this day.

9 The Metal Whistle

Quasimodo took Esmeralda to a little room near the bell tower. When she woke up from her faint, she found him staring at her.

"Why did you save me?" she asked.

He kept staring at her, trying to guess what she had said. Then he fled. He returned a short while later with food and a nun's white gown. "Eat!" he said.

The gypsy lifted her eyes to thank him. But she could not say a word. She hung her head in fear.

"You are afraid of me because I am so ugly," said Quasimodo. "Do not look at me; only listen. You must stay here. Do not try to leave the church. The soldiers will kill you."

She raised her head to answer, but the hunchback had limped away again. She looked around the room. It had just one door and a little window.

The next morning, a ray of sun came through the window and shone on the sleeping girl's face. She opened her eyes and then closed them in fear. She had seen Quasimodo staring at her through the window.

He said, "Don't be frightened. I am your friend. I

will hide myself behind the wall. You can open your eyes again."

Esmeralda got up and opened the door. The hunchback was crouched next to the wall.

"Come in," she said.

Quasimodo thought she was asking him to leave. He began limping away. She ran after him. She took his arm and brought him back. But he would not enter her room.

He said, "I am deaf. And you . . . you are so very beautiful!"

She could not say a word.

"Yes, I am deaf. But you can speak to me by signs. My master talks with me in that way. Soon I shall learn to read your lips."

He drew a small metal whistle from his pocket. He said, "This is for you. When you need me, whistle with this. It makes a high sound that I can hear."

Esmeralda took the whistle; Quasimodo then fled.

The days went by. The king still had not returned to Paris, so Esmeralda was safe. She saw no one but Quasimodo. She was an unhappy girl! No matter how hard she tried, she could not get used to him. He was too ugly.

One morning Esmeralda stood outside her room looking across the square. Quasimodo stood behind her. All at once she cried out, "Phoebus! Phoebus!"

Quasimodo looked down to where she was

pointing. He saw Phoebus tying his horse to a post. Then Phoebus entered the house of Fleur-de-Lys.

The hunchback understood at once. His eye filled with tears, but not one fell. "Shall I bring him to you?" he asked at last.

"Oh, yes! Go! Run, quick! Bring him to me!"

He ran down the stairs, choked with sobs. The horse was still tied to the post when he reached the square. The hunchback looked up and saw Esmeralda gazing down. Then he hid himself and waited for the captain to come out.

Quasimodo waited all day long and well into the night. Fleur-de-Lys was having a party to celebrate her coming wedding. Many guests came and went.

At last the captain left the house and mounted his horse. Quasimodo ran up and said, "Follow me, captain! The gypsy girl wants to see you!"

"The gypsy girl!" The captain put his hand on his sword.

The deaf man said, "Quick! Quick! This way!"

Phoebus kicked Quasimodo with all his might. The startled hunchback stepped back. In that instant, Phoebus dug his spurs into the horse. He galloped away in the darkness.

Quasimodo returned to Notre Dame. He lighted his lamp and climbed to the tower. Esmeralda was waiting for him to return.

"I could not find him," he said. She began to sob.

The gypsy saw no more of the hunchback after that day. Each morning she found food outside her door, but that was all. She thought often of her handsome captain.

During all this time, Frollo had been ill. He lay in bed with a high fever, dreaming of Esmeralda. He remembered how she had stared up at him as he stabbed the captain. Then he saw her faint as the captain's blood dripped on her bare throat. Most of all, he remembered how he had kissed her pale lips before fleeing out the window.

These memories heated his blood higher and

higher. The other priests thought he was going to die. However, one night he leapt from his bed and left his room. He carried a lamp in his hand.

Esmeralda was sleeping in her little room. As always, she was dreaming of Phoebus. She heard a noise and opened her eyes. There at her window she saw a face lighted by a lamp. Her eyes opened wide with fear.

A moment later she felt a hot touch. The priest had glided to her side. He blew out the lamp and held her in his arms. She tried to scream but could not. He pressed his lips to her shoulders.

The priest hissed, "My love for you is like fire! It is like a thousand knives driven into my heart!"

She struck him again and again.

"Love me! Love me!" cried the priest. He held her tightly.

"Help! Help!" she shrieked. But no one came.

"Silence!" said the priest.

Suddenly the gypsy touched a cold metal object on her bed. It was Quasimodo's whistle. She seized it and raised it to her lips. She blew it with all her strength. It made a sharp, high sound.

Suddenly a strong arm reached down and grabbed the priest. In a flash, Frollo was stretched out on the floor. He felt an oddly shaped knee pressed against his chest. The priest knew at once that it was Quasimodo's. But the room was dark.

Quasimodo did not know that it was his master who lay beneath him.

"Quasimodo!" yelled the priest. It was no use. Quasimodo could not see at all in the darkness.

The hunchback raised a knife and prepared to strike. Then he stopped. "No blood in her room!" he said. He grabbed the priest and dragged him outside. The moon shone faintly in the sky.

Quasimodo looked down and saw the priest's face. He let go of his master and fell back. Esmeralda had followed them outside. She saw that the two had changed places. Now it was the priest who was in control.

Frollo signaled Quasimodo to leave. But the hunchback stepped between the priest and the gypsy. He said, "My lord, do what you will. But kill me first." Then he held the knife out to the priest.

Yet the gypsy was quicker than Frollo. She tore the knife from Quasimodo's hand and held it high above her head. "You dare not touch me now, coward!" she cried. Then she added, "I know that Phoebus is not dead!"

The priest rushed away, quivering with rage. Quasimodo found the whistle on the ground and handed it back to Esmeralda. Then he, too, left.

The girl went back inside her room. She fell on her bed and burst into tears. Slowly but surely, her sanctuary was turning into a prison.

10 The Living Stones

The king of France returned to Paris at last. He ordered that Esmeralda's sanctuary end in three days.

When this news reached Frollo, he hurried out of the church in search of Pierre Gringoire. He found the poet not far away.

He said, "Pierre, Esmeralda will hang in three days. We must help her!"

Pierre answered, "Help her? Oh yes, I suppose so." He had been trying to forget all about Esmeralda. He no longer missed her, though he did wish to have the goat back. At last, he felt that he should do something to help.

Pierre finally spoke up. "I know! My friends in the Court of Miracles love her. They'll be happy to attack the church tomorrow night and carry her off!"

"An excellent plan," answered the priest. And the two of them talked in whispers for some time.

The next night a large crowd of vagrants gathered in a tavern on the Court of Miracles. Men, women, and children were heaped together, drinking and laughing. The king of thieves sat in one corner handing out axes, swords, and other weapons. He said, "Hurry! Arm yourselves! Get ready to march!"

Pierre Gringoire sat nearby, staring at the floor.

One of the drunken thieves jumped up on a table and yelled out, "Brothers and sisters! We are brave! We'll attack the church and break open the doors! We'll rescue the gypsy! We'll save her from the priests and the hunchback! Prepare for battle!"

"Midnight!" shouted their king.

Then the crowd rushed out onto the dark court. They formed a long line. The king marched to the front and said, "Silence! Not a word or a light until we reach Notre Dame!" With that, they began to march.

That night, as usual, Quasimodo closed and locked the huge front door of the church. With its thick iron bars, the door was as solid as a wall.

Quasimodo climbed to the balcony and looked across the square. No one had told him that Esmeralda's sanctuary would end the next day. But that day he had noticed evil-looking men prowling around the church.

As Quasimodo looked out, he saw a dark mass fill the square. It looked like an army of ghosts. He sensed that they had come to take the gypsy from him. He wondered if he should wake Esmeralda and try to escape with her. But the crowd covered the space on three sides of the church. There was no way to get through. The back of the church faced the river. But Quasimodo did not have the key to the back door. And besides, there was no boat.

There was only one thing to do. He let Esmeralda sleep and decided to face the crowd alone.

Down below, 30 men began working on the front door with hammers and crowbars. The door refused to budge.

"Courage, men!" shouted the king of thieves.

Just then, a huge wooden beam fell from the sky and crushed a dozen men. The others ran away in fear.

The king said, "It's the work of the devil! No matter! Forward, lads!"

The men looked at the dark church. Then they looked at the beam. None of them moved.

At last one man said, "Sir, our hammers are no good against the door."

"Then use the beam!" answered the king.

This idea gave the vagrants courage. A hundred men lifted the beam and slammed it against the door. But the door still did not budge. At the same time, a shower of large stones began falling on the men's heads.

The king asked, "Is the church itself fighting back? Don't stop now!"

Again and again, the men slammed the beam against the door. The whole cathedral shook. The door boomed like a drum, but still it held. Meanwhile, the stones kept falling.

The stones came from Quasimodo, as did the beam. He had found them in a storeroom in the tower. He had tipped the beam over the edge of the balcony with his incredible strength. Then he watched it fall on the crowd 160 feet below. Quasimodo had then thrown the stones, one by one, with deadly aim. Dead thieves lay all across the ground.

Still the men battered the door. They could feel it giving way. Then the stones stopped falling. They smashed the door once, twice, three times. They knew the next time would be the last. All of a sudden, a stream of molten lead poured down on the men. They shrieked with agony as this liquid fire burned them alive.

All eyes looked toward the balcony. At last they saw Quasimodo. He was lighted by the flames of a raging fire. He had found sheets of lead and was melting them over the fire. The crowd drew back in terror.

The king shouted, "We cannot enter by the door! Where is Gringoire? Maybe he knows another way!"

One of the men answered, "Sir, he disappeared as we were crossing the river."

The king said, "What the devil? He urges us on, and then he leaves us. He's a coward!"

Just then a vagrant came running up, dragging a long ladder. "We'll get in with this!" he yelled. A

dozen men helped him lean the ladder against a low porch below the balcony. They all climbed up at once. Just as the first man reached the top, two strong arms pushed the ladder backward. It tottered for an instant, then fell to the ground with a sickening thud.

This last sight filled the mob with fury. How could one man hold them off for so long? They found more ladders and attacked the church from all sides. Some used knotted ropes. Others climbed the walls.

There was no way to stop this raging crowd. Fury gleamed from their faces. They climbed higher and higher. They howled, panted, swore.

Quasimodo turned this way and that. He could no longer stop the mob. He watched them draw closer and closer. Then he turned his eye to the dark sky and began to pray. He feared for Esmeralda's life.

Suddenly, the sound of galloping horses filled the square. Hundreds of horsemen charged the crowd like a whirlwind, shouting "France! France! The king's men to the rescue!" At their head rode Captain Phoebus, his sword flashing. The terrified vagrants turned to fight this new enemy.

Quasimodo heard nothing. But he saw the swords, the horsemen, and Captain Phoebus. Finding new strength, he ran in every direction, pushing ladders away and hurling men to their deaths.

Down in the square, the vagrants fought bravely. They swung their axes and torches. But the horsemen answered with swords and spears. Blood flowed like water. Captain Phoebus rode like a hero through it all. His sword brought death again and again.

At last most of the vagrants ran for their lives. Their dead lay in heaps across the square.

Quasimodo cleared the last vagrant from the church. Then he looked down to see the horsemen's victory. He fell on his knees and raised his hands to heaven. Mad with joy, he ran to Esmeralda's room. Now she was all he could think of.

He entered her room at last. She was gone.

11 The Little Shoe

Esmeralda had been asleep when the vagrants attacked the church. But quickly the noise of the attack had wakened her. She sat up, listened, and looked around. Djali began bleating. What new terror must Esmeralda face? She lay in her bed, trembling.

Soon Esmeralda heard footsteps outside her door. Two men entered her room. One was covered in black from head to foot. He carried a lantern. The other was Pierre Gringoire.

"Pierre!" she said. "Who is that with you?"

"Do not fear," answered Gringoire. "He is a friend of mine."

The poet bent down to pet Djali. He was so happy to see the goat again! He could make lots of money with this goat, he thought.

The man in black gave Gringoire a shove. Gringoire said, "I almost forgot. We must hurry, Esmeralda. Your life is in danger—and Djali's too. They want to hang you again. We are your friends. We have come to save you. Follow us."

"Why doesn't your friend speak?" asked the gypsy.

"He cannot."

She did not believe Gringoire. But she let the men lead her away. She had no choice.

They walked down the stairs and toward the back of the church. Behind them, the beam crashed into the main door again and again. They came to the back door. The man in black opened it with a key. On the other side was the Seine.

The man in black walked along the river to a large bush. There he pulled out a hidden rowboat. Gringoire and Esmeralda stepped in, followed by Djali. The man in black got in last. He sat down in the front of the boat. Then he began rowing to the other side of the river. The Greve was located there.

Gringoire sat in the back and took the goat on his knees. The gypsy sat next to him. Gringoire said, "Oh, we are saved!"

The boat moved slowly across the water. All at once, torches lighted the church behind them. Then they heard soldiers shouting, "The gypsy! Where is the gypsy? Death to the gypsy!"

The poor girl hid her face in her hands. The man in black rowed faster. Meanwhile, Gringoire thought to himself, making plans. He hugged the goat closer in his arms. Then he slowly edged away from the gypsy.

The boat reached the other side of the river with a jolt. The man in black tried to take Esmeralda's hand, but she stepped back. Meanwhile, Gringoire pushed her away. She ended up jumping to the shore by herself. In the confusion, Gringoire slipped away with the goat. Esmeralda stood alone on the shore with the man in black.

The gypsy shuddered. She tried to call out to Gringoire, but no sound came from her lips. All at once she felt the man's hand on her arm. It was a cold, strong hand. He walked toward the Greve, pulling her along.

Soon they stood at the Greve. The gypsy could see the pillory and the gallows in the middle of the square. The man stopped in front of her. He pulled the hood off his face. It was Frollo.

He looked like a ghost. He said, "Listen! We have reached our goal. Your life is in my hands. The king has ordered you back to the gallows. Even now his men are searching for you. Look!"

He pointed toward the church. The torches of the soldiers were drawing nearer. "Death to the gypsy!" they shouted.

"You see that I am not lying," he went on. "I have saved you. Everything is ready. It is for you to choose."

Then he ran to the gallows, pulling her after him. He pointed at it. "Choose between the gallows and me," he said.

Esmeralda tore herself from him. Then she fell at

the foot of the gallows. She turned her lovely head and looked at him. At last she said, "You are more horrible than the gallows."

The priest grabbed her and began laughing wildly. "You must die, my beauty, or be mine! Kiss me, foolish girl! My bed or the tomb!"

She screamed, "Let me go! It is Phoebus I love! Phoebus alone is handsome. You, priest, are old! You are ugly! Begone!"

"Then die!" he said. And he dragged her toward the rat hole.

Quickly they reached the iron bars of the tiny cell. The priest called out, "Sister Gudule! Here is the gypsy girl. Hold her well!"

The nun's hand came through the bars. She held the gypsy's wrist with an iron grip.

The priest said, "It's the gypsy witch. Do not let her go. I will fetch the officers. You shall see her hanged."

The nun laughed at these bloody words. The priest ran toward the soldiers at Notre Dame.

Panting with terror, the girl tried to free herself. But the nun held her like an iron clamp. The nun's hand seemed chained to her wrist.

Esmeralda sank back and felt the fear of death. She thought of the beauty of life and of her love for Phoebus. Then she looked at the gallows in the middle of the square.

"Ha! ha! ha! You shall be hanged!" said the nun.

The gypsy looked the nun straight in the face. "What have I done to you?" she asked weakly.

"You are a gypsy! You are one of the people who stole my child! I have prayed for 15 years. I have not left this hole for 15 years. Now I will have my revenge!"

Dawn was breaking slowly over the square. Esmeralda thought she heard horsemen coming. She was crazy with fright. She wailed, "Have pity! Let me go! I cannot die!"

"Give me back my child!" said the nun.

Esmeralda answered, "How strange. You seek your child, and I seek my parents."

The nun kept holding on to Esmeralda with one hand. She reached into her gown with the other hand and pulled out a little shoe. She held the shoe before the gypsy and said, "Do you see this? It is all I have left of my child."

"My God!" cried Esmeralda. "My God!" And with her free hand she ripped open the green bag that hung around her neck. It contained the mate to the little pink shoe.

"My daughter!" the nun cried out.

"Mother!" cried the gypsy.

And the two grabbed each other through the bars. Then the nun said, "Quick! Get inside! You will be safe here."

The window was the only entrance to the tiny cell. The rusty bars that crossed the window were cemented in place. The nun took a stone and smashed the bars. They broke easily. Then she hauled her daughter in. She fit the bars back over the window as well as she could.

Just then, horsemen entered the Greve. The hangman was among them. He said, "Over here. The priest said we would find her at the rat hole."

"Hide in the corner!" whispered the nun. The gypsy crawled into the darkest corner of the tiny cell. She could not be seen through the window.

The hangman came to the window. He asked,

"Where is the gypsy? We are here to hang her."

The nun answered, "She bit me. I had to let her go."

"And which way did she run?" the hangman asked.

"Down that street over there," said the nun, pointing.

The hangman looked at her hand. As he did, he noticed the twisted and broken window bars. "What happened to these bars?" he asked.

"A cart backed into them yesterday," answered the nun.

"I think you're lying," said the hangman.

One of the horsemen said, "Sir, this woman hates gypsies. She has no reason to lie."

The hangman said, "All right. Let's go." And he began to walk away.

Just then, another horseman spoke. He said, "I can't waste my time looking for gypsies. They need me back at the cathedral. Go on without me." And he rode off.

It was the voice of Captain Phoebus! Before she could even think, Esmeralda called out his name. But he had already gone.

The hangman, however, heard her. He rushed back to the cell. He pulled out the bars and called out, "Ha! Two rats in the trap!"

The nun picked up the stone and tried to smash

the hangman's head. But he was too quick for her. He stepped back. Then he ordered the horsemen to make the window larger. They found pickaxes and set right to work. Soon the window was the size of a door.

The nun threw herself across the opening. She sobbed, "She is my daughter! My daughter! Please do not take her from me! For 15 years, I thought she was dead. But now God has given me a miracle! She is alive! You cannot hang her now!"

The horsemen stayed back. Some were moved to tears. But the hangman was firm. "It is the king's command," he said. And he entered the cell.

The poor mother threw herself on top of her daughter. The hangman reached down and dragged them both out of the cell. By this time, a large crowd had already gathered to watch the hanging. Across the river, a tall priest watched from the north tower of Notre Dame.

The hangman dragged the two women across the square. At last he reached the ladder at the foot of the gallows. He flung the mother away from her child with one quick pull. The mother staggered back and fell to the ground. Then the hangman placed a rope around Esmeralda's neck. He put his foot on the ladder.

Suddenly, the mother leapt on him and bit his hand. Soldiers ran to his aid. They pulled his bleeding hand from between the mother's teeth. Then they pushed her away again. This time she fell to the ground with a thud. They lifted her up, but she fell back again. She was dead.

The hangman, still carrying Esmeralda, began to climb the ladder.

12 The Marriage of Quasimodo

Quasimodo found Esmeralda's room empty when he returned from battling the vagrants. He stamped his foot with surprise and rage. Then he began running all over the church searching for the gypsy girl. He was soon joined by the king's troops. Together they covered every inch of the church. Quasimodo did not know that the troops wanted to hang the gypsy. He showed them every corner of the church. There was no Esmeralda.

Soon the troops left, but Quasimodo kept searching. He ran everywhere calling for her. He poked his head into every hole. Finally, when he was sure that she was gone, he slowly climbed the stairs to the north tower. They were the same stairs he had climbed on the day he saved her life. He passed by all the same places. But this time his head hung down with sadness.

The church was empty. The troops were now searching for Esmeralda in the streets of Paris. Quasimodo returned to the gypsy's empty room. He threw himself against the wall and fell fainting to the floor.

When he awoke, the hunchback flung himself on the bed. He rolled on it. He kissed the place where the young girl had slept. He beat his head against the wall. At last he dragged himself out of the room on his knees. He knelt outside the room for more than an hour. He stared at the empty space. He did not say a word. His body shook with sobs.

During this time, Quasimodo began thinking about his master, Frollo. He remembered how his master had attacked Esmeralda just a few days before. He began to think that Frollo must have been the one who just stole the gypsy.

Just as the hunchback was thinking these thoughts, he saw Frollo walking toward him. The priest was headed for the tower, but he kept looking across the river. He did not even see the hunchback as he walked by. Frollo began climbing the stairs that led to the very top of the tower. Quasimodo rose and followed him. He did not know why. He was full of fury and full of fear.

Quasimodo quickly reached the top of the tower. The priest was standing with his back to his servant. He was leaning on the railing, looking across the river. He was staring so hard that he did not hear Quasimodo come up behind him.

The sun had just risen. The sky was clear. Down below, people were beginning to stir. Smoke rose from the chimneys. Carts rolled down the streets.

Workers swung hammers. The river looked like silver in the morning light.

In the square below the cathedral, people pointed to the battered door and to the pools of lead. These were the only lasting signs of the battle. The soldiers had already thrown the dead bodies into the river and washed away the blood.

But the priest saw none of this. His eyes were fixed on a single point. Quasimodo looked there as well. Thus he saw what the priest saw. It was the gallows in the Greve.

A man was climbing the ladder to the gallows. Across his shoulder, he was carrying a young girl dressed in white, with a rope around her neck. Quasimodo looked more closely. The girl was Esmeralda!

Just then the hangman reached the top of the ladder. He tightened the rope around the gypsy's neck. All at once he pushed her away. The poor girl dangled from the end of the rope, a dozen feet above the ground. Then a horrible shudder ran through her body. Her neck was broken. She was dead.

At that instant an awful laugh broke from the priest's lips. Quasimodo did not hear this laugh, but he saw it. The hunchback stepped back a few paces. Then he rushed upon the priest. He lifted Frollo into the air and threw him over the railing.

Just below the railing was a gutter. Frollo grabbed

onto this as he fell. He clung there to life. Above him was the angry face of Quasimodo. Two hundred feet below him was the hard ground—and death.

Quasimodo did not even look at the archdeacon. Instead, he leaned on the railing, staring at the gallows. A river of tears flowed from his eye.

Meanwhile Frollo gasped. The gutter began to bend. It was not strong enough to hold him. His fingers began to slip. His arms grew weaker and weaker.

Frollo looked again at the weeping Quasimodo and at the ground far below. He tried to lift himself up, but it was no use. He could no longer hold on. He let go.

Quasimodo watched the priest fall. As he fell, he turned over and over. Then he smashed into the hard stones far below. His body was still.

The hunchback raised his eye to the gypsy again. She swung gently from the gallows in her pure white gown. Then he looked down at the figure in the black robe. It had no trace of human shape.

Quasimodo sobbed and said, "Oh, all that I ever loved!"

By that evening Quasimodo had vanished from Notre Dame. The soldiers who removed the priest's twisted body could find no trace of the hunchback. He was never seen again.

Later that night, workers took Esmeralda's body down from the gallows. They carried her body outside the city to the mass grave at Montfauçon.

The grave was a stone building 15 feet high, 30 feet wide, and 40 feet long. The bodies from all the gallows in Paris were thrown into it, where they lay one on top of another, slowly rotting.

The workers threw Esmeralda's body into the mass grave and then returned to the city.

Nearly two years later, another group of workers came to the grave at Montfauçon. There they found two skeletons locked together among all of the dead bodies. One skeleton was that of a woman. Around her neck was a necklace with an empty green bag. The other was that of a man. His spine was curved, and one leg was shorter than the other. His neck was not broken; he had not been hanged.

It was decided that the man must have come to the grave and died there, holding the woman. When the workers tried to loosen him from the woman's skeleton, his body crumbled into dust.